COMPOST THIS BOOK

AF005896

COMPOST THIS BOOK

CASSANDRA MARKETOS

APOGEE GRAPHICS

CONTENTS

HELLO	7
ETHOS	11
HISTORY	13
WHERE TO PUT A COMPOST	17
HOW TO COMPOST	21
HOW TO USE COMPOST	25
WHAT YOU SHOULD COMPOST	29
(MICRO)BIOLOGY-CHEMISTRY	33
COMPOSTING IN SMALL SPACES	37
VERMICOMPOST	41
WHAT YOU SHOULDN'T COMPOST	45
COMPOST THIS BOOK	49

HELLO

When I first started composting, I had no idea what I was doing. I didn't know what compost was, exactly, or how to make it "work." Vague memories of my mom's enormous backyard pile contained only the size of certain lizards and that flies are sometimes a problem. Google searching was surprisingly difficult. There wasn't a ton of straightforward information available. Different sites used different terms, rules, and ratios. Things seemed overwhelmingly technical and there were a lot of percentages involved. I was warned about animals and odors. "Don't compost citrus" seemed to be a hard rule.

But why?

Eventually, I gave up and just started piling food in a corner of my yard (including citrus peels). I buried this food in leaf litter, wet it down, and let it be. After that, I would take a fresh bowl of food scraps out about once a week, dig a small hole in the center of my pile, place the scraps inside, and bury them using fresh leaf litter and other yard waste. Sometimes, I would just cover the pile in dirt. It rained often that winter, keeping the pile consistently and reasonably moist.

After some time passed, I began to notice things. If my pile lacked a certain amount of grass and leaves or twigs, my food scraps wouldn't decay. Instead, they would clump together, become slimy, and start to smell. I started keeping my pile at an intuitive ratio of yard waste to food scraps. If the pile got too dry, decay also seemed to slow. If it didn't rain enough, I'd supplement with a hose. A little after that, I began to notice that no matter how much new food and yard waste I added, my pile wasn't seeming to get bigger. Instead, it was decaying at an even clip with what was being added. It was also emitting an odor. Not a gross odor, like rotting food, but a good odor. A dark, rich, earthy smell. Worms were starting to appear. Not just under the pile, but all across my tiny garden. My compost had worked.

These days, I know more about decomposition. Enough to understand, more scientifically, why my original observations were so accurate. I know about nitrogen and carbon ratios and why different things decompose at different rates. I know which bacteria are at work and when, and why it's a good thing if beetles start to appear. I know that it's fine to compost citrus, although I may never understand why people are so concerned about orange peels. I know that a good pile, well-tended, will not attract animals and it won't stink. But, most importantly, I know that composting doesn't have to be difficult or even particularly complex. You can just go ahead and do it, armed with just your eyes and your nose, and a little bit of common sense.

I made this book because I wanted to help other people feel the same. I wanted to give them a way to get started that wasn't prescriptive, complex, or even particularly scientific—even though I love science. My composting methodology is about what we can learn simply by noticing; it's not about memorizing rules, but developing a relationship to your own particular pile.

These days, I love my compost. It's filled with pill bugs, black beetles, worms, and even tiny salamanders. Under a microscope, it's positively luminous; dozens of tiny creatures skipping about in their enviable work of turning my trash into living, fertile soil. A handful of my compost, patted around the base of a growing vegetable plant, will cause it to bloom overnight, limbs raised and leaves spreading with new and magnificent vigor.

What you're holding in your hands right now might be the only version of itself to ever exist, and when you're done I am going to instruct you on how to turn it into compost. What's more beautiful than that?

Open air compost, 2021
Mushroom blocks, loose grass, oyster shells,
coffee grounds, food scraps

ETHOS

DON'T HIDE YOUR COMPOST. In order to make your compost good, you need to be able to get to know it. What do you see? What do you smell? Is the pile crumbly and dry? Is it slimy? These simple and observable features will help you make small adjustments, over time, to what you add and when you turn, so that you can work your way toward an ideal pile.

EVERYTHING ORGANIC DECAYS. It will decay whether you put it in a pile or flat on the ground, it will decay whether you mix it up with other stuff or leave it alone, and it will decay whether you turn it every day or don't touch it for a whole year. "Compost" means that you, a human, are intersecting with this process to help things decay a little more deliberately, perhaps with less smells or while attracting fewer animals.

KNOW THY PILE, KNOW THYSELF. Your work is to develop a relationship to your particular pile, so that it meets your specific and particular needs. Do you need your compost for a garden? Then you may want to make sure things decay on a timeline. Are you worried about smells because you have neighbors nearby? Then you'll want to be fastidious about covering your food scraps with lots of leaves and perhaps build an enclosure. Are bears a problem? Then put your compost far from the house. Do you just want to get rid of your food scraps in an environmentally-friendly way? Then you can do pretty much anything you want.

RELAX. Spreadsheets, precise ratios and measurements... These can be wonderful tools for compost if you're a farmer. They can help you make maximally nutritious compost in the least amount of time and a lot of people I love and admire are very knowledgeable and successful composters of this variety. Not everybody needs to be a scientist about compost, though. You—the person reading this—probably do not. That's why the first thing I tell each of my classes is: "relax." Life is tough enough. Compost never should be.

HISTORY

Every culture has used compost in some form, many dating back thousands and thousands of years. The earliest written record of compost is on a set of clay tablets from the Akkadian Empire, which existed in the Mesopotamian Valley one thousand years before Moses was born. Ancient Hindu texts reference composting. In China, a composting method involving oil cake amended with crop residue was recorded by Chen Fu around the year 1149. Ancient Greeks composted. In the *Oeconomicus*, a Socratic dialogue concerned with household management and agriculture, the Greek warrior and philosopher Xenophon advised farmers to gather weeds and allow them to rot in water, in order to create a green manure for the improvement of their fields. Plutarch, another Greek philosopher, observed that the rotting of human bodies after war was productive for growing food:

They say that the soil, after the bodies had rotted and the winter rains had fallen, was so fertilized and saturated with the putrefied matter which sank into it, that it produced an unusual crop the next season.[1]

Early Hebrew scripture references manure being mixed with street sweepings and organic refuse, part of a dunghill that was kept at the edge of the city. The Talmud describes how "They lay dung to moisten and enrich the soil; dig about the roots of trees; pluck up the seckers; take off the leaves; sprinkle ashes; and smoke under the trees to kill vermin."[2] Cleopatra, in 50 B.C., is reported to have made worms sacred after observing their composting abilities. She enacted laws to make their removal from Egypt a crime punishable by death.

George Washington has been referred to as America's first composter, but he wasn't. Per the historian Jim Loewen, "Composting first appears in the historical record of what is now the United States in 1621, when Squanto showed the 'Pilgrims' how to put a fish in each corn hill, so the maize and squash would thrive." He goes on to describe how different pieces of indigenous language outlined the use and meaning of compost for native peoples: "Narragansetts called the fish 'munnawhatteaûgs,' which means 'fertilizer' or 'that which enriches the land',' a word the English corrupted into 'menhaden.' The Abenakis of Maine called them 'pauhagens,' which also means 'fertilizer,' a name the English shortened to 'pogies.'"[3]

Later, John Adams was so enthusiastic about compost that his frequent mentions of manure were actually struck from his diaries before their initial publication.

They appeared in later editions, though:

> In one of my common Walks, along the Edgeware Road, there are fine Meadows belonging to a noted cow keeper. These Plotts are plentifully manured. There are on the Side of the Way, several heaps of manure, an hundred Loads perhaps in each heap. I have carefully examined them and find them composed of Straw and dung from the Stables and Streets of London, mud, Clay or Marl, dug out of the Ditch along the Hedge and Turf, Sward cutt up, with Spades, hoes and hovels in the Road. This may be good manure, but it is not equal to mine.[4]

Recently, a friend wrote to me about "witches" in medieval France who built homes with compost roofs, meant for both warmth and protection. I tried in vain to search for more information on these fertile covens, but Google turned up blank after blank. Eventually, he wrote to his friend (an "anarchist," he said), and asked for her to repeat the story. "*Los Evangiles des Ecreignes,* I think," she wrote back. "But I'm camping and will have to look more when I'm home."

I searched the phrase on Google, and translated the results. Months later I returned to them to try and remember. They read only: "Tea women of the people, who never yielded."

July 8. Saturday. in one of my common Walks, along the Edgeware Road, there are fine Meadows, or Squares of grass Land belonging to a noted Cow keeper. These Plotts are plentifully manured. There are on the Side of the way, Several heaps of Manure an hundred Loads perhaps in each heap. I have carefully examined them and find them composed of Straw, and dung from the Stables and Streets of London, mud, Clay, or Marl, dug out of the Ditch, along the Hedge, and Turf, Sward cut up, with Spades, hoes & Shovels in the Road. This is laid in vast heaps to mix.

John Adams, Diary 44, July 8, 1786

WHERE TO PUT A COMPOST

"Where should I put my compost pile?" is a question that nags most compost newbies that I work with. Should they put it in the shade? What about the sun? Does it need a lot of space? What about animals? These are all good questions, but they neglect to address the single, most important factor regarding the success of any given compost heap: you. As the composter, your own physical abilities and daily routines should be the first point of consideration when determining the ideal location of your pile.

I've "fixed" many composts by simply relocating them, making the heap more accessible to the daily routine of the composter. One woman I worked with had her heap placed on the far side of her rather generously-sized property. "I know I love to compost, but I just don't ever seem to add my food scraps to the pile," she lamented, as we made the five-minute walk from her house to where her heap resided.

"It's a mystery!"

It was not a mystery.

If this woman was going to use her compost, her pile needed to be closer to the place where she spent her time cooking. I gathered her compost and moved it into a simple stone enclosure just outside of her back door. The woman's compost practice flourished soon after.

Another friend told me his compost was "broken" and asked if I might check it out. When I arrived on his property, I found that he'd piled his heap into a very tall and narrow chicken-wire enclosure, making turning a clumsy and onerous procedure. As a result, decomposition had essentially halted. I cut open the chicken wire and re-circled it, adding about three feet in diameter to the heap. A little more space made turning the pile much easier and so he stopped putting it off.

A week later, his compost was humming along at a neat and active 110°F.

I often encounter this problem of "mysterious" neglect when people build their compost in out-of-the-way places or have cumbersome set ups that make basic interaction a challenge. It becomes hard to develop a new habit. Your pile will thrive when you locate it in a place where you can see and interact with it easily, and when you build it in a way that allows its maintenance to align with your abilities. That's why I joke with people that making your first compost is a little like going to therapy. In order for it to work, you need to look within—not, necessarily, toward some locatable set of stable, external factors.

In general, having your compost pile located in a place that you see and will be regularly around acts as a reminder to care. It also helps you learn. Your day-to-day observations will teach you all kinds of things about your heap: what smells and what doesn't, what combinations will decay more quickly than others, what inputs you need more or less of, and how fast decomposition is occurring. You will be amazed at how quickly you learn the language of your pile when you look at it every day.

Not everyone has access to so much space that their only compost concern is their own preferences, though. Living in cities means living with other people and it's important to take them into consideration. For example: if your ideal compost location ends up being directly beneath the bedroom window of a neighbor, you may want to rethink your approach. You could also have a conversation with them. You may just make a new compost friend.

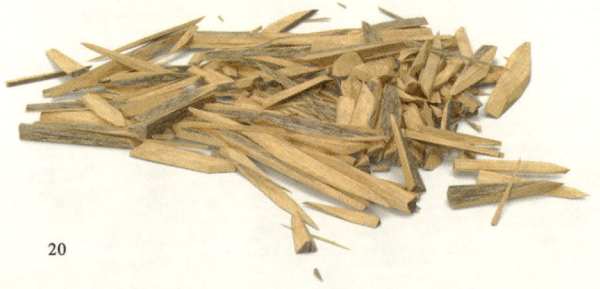

HOW TO COMPOST

All compost is composed of four basic elements: nitrogen, carbon, water, and oxygen. Nitrogen comes from food scraps, green grass clippings, and animal manure. Carbon comes from dry and woody matter, like dead leaves and wood chips. Oxygen comes from turning your pile and/or incorporating sturdy carbon materials throughout your heap in order to provide aeration and prevent compaction. Water comes from rain, a hose, or your kitchen sink.

To build your compost pile, you'll simply want to find a location and heap all of these components together. If you have a backyard or access to any outdoor area, that can be in the form of a big open-air compost heap or a trench you've dug in the ground or inside of a compost bin that you've purchased at the store. If you live in an apartment, it can simply be inside of a plastic bag that you stash under the sink.

No matter where you're building a compost pile, though, it helps to get started by alternating layers of carbon and nitrogen. Lay a base down of wood chips or dried twigs and dead leaves. (This helps reduce compaction as your pile grows and gets heavier.) Then, add some food scraps. Then add some more dead leaves. Then add a little bit more food scraps, and so on. Your overall pile should be balanced in favor of carbon—more carbon than nitrogen. Add three handfuls of carbon for every handful of nitrogen. When you're finished, wet the pile. An ideal pile is moist throughout, but not sopping wet.

If you're up for it, you can also break everything down into the tiniest bits possible. Doing this will really expedite the speed of decomposition in your pile. Chop food scraps up. Break twigs in half. Shred leaves and chop grass.

Your job is now to keep the components of your pile balanced, over time. You'll want to keep your ratio of carbon to nitrogen about the same, and the pile persistently damp. Doing this does not have to be complicated. Add a little nitrogen each time you add carbon, and add carbon each time you add nitrogen. For example, if you're adding a big bowl of food scraps from last night's dinner (nitrogen), throw in a few handfuls of dead leaves (carbon), at the same time or soon after. Personally, I like to dig a small hole in the top of my pile each time I add new food scraps, and then cover them with leaves or twigs.

If you're raking leaves in your yard and want to add them all to your compost heap at once, incorporate them into the pile with some water or an extra batch of food scraps. You can also set them aside and use them slowly throughout the course of the year, grabbing a few handfuls each time you need to add fresh food scraps.

From time-to-time, you'll also want to turn your compost. This brings all the material on the outer and upper edges of your compost into the center and bottom, which ensures everything has a chance to break down. It also aids with ongoing aeration. Most composters will turn their piles every four to five weeks. If your compost starts to get hot, you can turn as frequently as every two weeks. You also don't have to turn it... ever. It will take longer, but it will still break down and become compost.

Compost trench, 2023
Flowers, citrus peels, dried leaves, fermenting plums

HOW TO USE COMPOST

There's no test you can run on your compost that will make it ding and say: "I'm finished!" There are, however, a set of simple questions you can ask and observations you can make that will give you a near-indisputable reading.

> *What do you see?* Your compost should be dark and crumbly, a lot like soil. Put your hand into your pile and sift it through your fingers. If there are still patches of slime or visible and "undigested" food scraps, your compost isn't ready yet. Let it keep sitting. If you have bulky twigs or wood chips remaining, though, that's fine. What you really want to avoid is any still-rotting food.

> *What do you smell?* Compost that is ready to be used smells like fresh, good earth. This smell is very

obvious. Once my friend Vivian came over and stepped onto my back porch, just as I opened up my pile for turning. "What smells so amazing?!?" she screamed. Your compost is ready when it smells good. It should not smell like ammonia or like anything is rotting.

What do you feel? If the pile is warm to the touch, that means that decomposition is still active and you want to avoid putting actively-decaying compost around your plants. Compost that is ready to use should be cool to the touch.

There are lots of ways you can put your finished compost to use. You can amend your soil, prepare a garden bed, fertilize mature plants, or start seedlings. To be honest, it's a little hard to mess this part up. Just so long as you are using compost, I think you're doing great.

AMEND YOUR SOIL. You can use your finished compost to add a burst of healthy microbes and fungi to your soil, which will help it with all kinds of things like water retention, nutrient cycling, and even carbon drawdown. You can do this pretty much anytime you want, and with whatever compost you have available. Just lay the compost down on top of the earth, wet it with a hose or (if you're water-conscious, which you should be) wait for rain, and let things be. I like to do this in "forgotten" spots around the yard, like crevices between asphalt. Some experts will recommend tilling compost into the soil and you certainly can, but there are trade offs to consider. Breaking up the existing earth will disturb networks of mycorrhizal fungi and, perhaps, valuable biological crusts. However, if you're using your compost on a particularly degraded or highly compacted area, the benefits of tilling and integration will probably outweigh the cons of any potential disruption. Use your best judgment.

PREPARE A GARDEN BED. Till one inch of compost to a depth of five inches in your future garden bed. I recommend doing this a few months in advance of planting, in order to give time for the microbes to "settle in." However, you can get away with as little time as seven days or so. Also, if you don't know what "one inch" of compost looks like or how to measure five inches... that's fine. Follow the blanket principle: mix some compost into your garden bed, in advance of actual planting.

PLANT SOMETHING. Throw a pinch or more of finished compost into the hole where you're about to transplant something.

DRESS YOUR VEGETABLES UP. Even if you've prepared your garden bed in advance with compost, your plants can still benefit from an additional compost-y boost as they grow. You don't need to use much. Add to the top of the soil in a thin layer, avoiding direct contact with stems. Different plants have different feeding needs, and you may want to adjust how much you use based on what you're planting.

PERK UP A HOUSEPLANT. Mix a handful of compost into your regularly purchased soil when potting or re-potting a houseplant. I've seen it recommended to use one part compost to three parts soil, but I'm generally imprecise and highly unscientific so I just say "a handful."

There's one other thing you can do and this one might be my personal favorite: give your compost away. I bet you that your local elementary school, community garden, old folks home, or whoever else would love a donation. Your neighbor might like some, your friends might like some— just ask around and see.

There's also, of course, the option of just never using your compost. You can spend ten years on a pile and never use an inch of it and it's still better for you and your environment for having done so.

WHAT YOU SHOULD COMPOST

In my opinion, almost anything is worth at least trying to compost, and a lot of the rumors you hear about what you "absolutely shouldn't" put in your pile (citrus, egg shells), are frankly untrue, albeit likely came from well-intentioned gardeners who saw that some things are harder to break down and/or more likely to attract animals. I appreciate their concern, but also want to encourage all brave and enterprising new composters to experiment freely and learn the lessons and preferences of their own pile. If you're nervous, you can segment your compost in order to experiment without risking "contamination" of the parent pile. You can also just throw everything together and see what happens. The fun of compost is that it's entirely up to you. What you put in your pile is your choice, based on how much time and energy you have, and contingent on what you plan to do with the finished product. Most stuff ends up working out, i.e. it eventually decays. (You will, too, one day.)

One thing to consider, when weighing what to add, though, is whether or not you have hot compost. If your pile is thermophilic (consistently above ~105°F, but honestly I feel best at about ~140°F), that means bad stuff like pathogens are more likely to just get cooked out. So, here is my unofficial list of things you should add to your pile, even if you're definitely-maybe-sort-of not supposed to:

CITRUS PEELS. Citrus is a great source of nitrogen, which any heap needs. It also offers phosphorus and potassium, which your future plants—if you use your compost to garden—will love. There are some things to be aware of when adding citrus, like how dumping ten pounds of lemon peels in at once will increase the overall acidity of your pile. You can avoid this by adding them in balanced portions with other types of food scraps, or covering them with a good, bulky carbon material like dead leaves. Yum.

EGGSHELLS. Eggshells are a fantastic add to any pile. They are a great source of calcium, and can help adjust your overall pH if your compost is on the acidic side. They do take awhile to break down if you add them without crushing or grinding them first, though.

PEE. I love telling people to pee on their piles because, at heart, I am seven. But seriously, urine is high in nitrogen and can function as a fantastic compost activator. If your pile isn't decaying at a good clip and you want to help speed things up, go ahead and piss on it. Pee can be especially helpful if your pile is heavy on carbon (dead leaves, wood chips). I manage the compost pile at a friend's house, and after filling the bin with yard waste from where we cleared out space for a garden, I told him to take a whiz on top. Two weeks later, the bulky leaves and weedy grasses had almost entirely disappeared.

HAIR. It takes a minute to break down, but hair slowly releases nitrogen into the pile as it decays, providing your heap with a steady source of a critical chemical. This applies to all kinds of hair too. Human hair, dog fur, cat hairballs, etc.

NAILS. Also a great source of slow-release nitrogen. Bonus: if you clip your nails directly over your pile, it will weird out your terrible neighbor who's always spying on you, and they'll stop.

WEEDS. You can compost weeds, but it's best done if your pile is consistently above 140°F. If a few weed seeds end up in your finished compost, though, you won't die and they won't ruin your compost. They just may sprout again if you use that compost in your garden, but nothing prevents you from simply weeding them out at that time.

ONIONS. You can definitely compost onions. They can rot and smell extremely bad, though, so add them deep in your pile, and make sure they're covered with a good mixture of browns (sawdust, soil, leaves).

(MICRO)BIOLOGY-CHEMISTRY

Your pile is full of microbes. Principle among them are aerobic bacteria, oxygen-loving microorganisms that break down organic matter in your pile. As these oxygen-loving microorganisms break down the organic matter in your pile, they turn it into fuel for their own cellular processes, which creates heat energy. (This is why some composts get hot.)

There are two main temperature ranges in composting: mesophilic and thermophilic. A mesophilic pile is between 50°F and 113°F. A thermophilic pile is anything above 113°F. The temperature of your pile is a big part in determining its particular population of microorganisms. A mesophilic pile is full of mesophiles, and a thermophilic pile is full of thermophiles. Go figure. Many backyard piles are permanently mesophilic. That's okay. Mesophiles can do the work of decomposition just fine, even if a little bit slower. However, most compost piles will vacillate between being mesophilic and thermophilic. Activity from mesophilic organisms will begin to steadily heat the pile, until the temperature gets too hot for them, at which point thermophiles take over. Thermophilic microorganisms love heat and can survive very high temperatures. They go to town until they run out of the type of high-energy material found in organic matter, at which time the temperature begins to decrease, and mesophilic organisms resume dominance. Thermophilic activity is most likely to occur right after you've added fresh materials.

Having "hot compost" is a badge of honor for some composters. It takes a practiced hand to achieve, it decomposes faster, and it has the added benefit of killing off pathogens, weed seeds, and other unmentionables that might have made it into your pile. If you're stuck wondering why your heap isn't getting hot enough, double-check what size you're keeping it at. For a pile to become thermophilic, it generally needs to be big enough to self-insulate (trap the heat that the aerobic bacteria are generating).

Your compost does not have to be hot to be "good," though. Many of my favorite piles are mesophilic. They are slow and cool, and they work just fine. I think often of this comment I saw in the subreddit r/composting:

> I used to be all for speed, grinding and mixing everything up to get hot as soon as possible. But then I noticed forest frogs moving in to near the pile in the summer and the previous owner of the house told me about a family of hedgehogs that always overwinter in the pile in the winter. Both of these are highly beneficial to the garden since we have a bad slug infestation (I'm in

South Sweden and it's a specific invasive species) and I started to take things slower with the compost and paying more attention to all the life around it. I still get to make almost more than I can use in the garden every year since I compost everything I can and love the process but speed is not really a priority anymore.

Personally, my own compost pile is steadily mesophilic and I love it. I find the undirected pace of decay both inspiring and soothing, and I don't do much to mess with it—more steward than commander of its secret and internal processes. People are sometimes surprised by this. Not that I would get attached to my compost, but the varied and flexible spectrum of what encompasses "compost," altogether. Compost can be a systemic and vigorous affair, with specific ratios, temperatures, preparations and maintenance. It can also be, simply put, slow. For practical reasons, you might even covet a slow compost.

When you compost "slowly"—leaving your compost undisturbed for long stretches of time—you give your pile a chance to mature beyond the initial, bacterially-driven phase of decomposition, and to progress toward fungal domination. A compost with good fungal content is able to break down different and hardier materials than a compost "stuck" in the bacterial phase due to consistent turning. It is also ideal for fertilizing mature trees and shrubs, or for improving the health of your soil. All those developed fungal threads expand the nutrient-cycling capacity of your dirt, making more food and water more available to your plants.

So: hot or cold, fast or slow.

There are no bad options with compost.

COMPOSTING IN SMALL SPACES

In my experience, the obstacles to small-space composting are more spiritual than practical. Composting indoors costs little money, takes few materials, and can be done with relative ease, but would-be practitioners are dogged by some familiar concerns: odors, animals, and a general aversion to "gross"-ness. The difference for the small-space dweller is one of proximity. If you're worried about a compost stinking, it makes a big difference if you're imagining that compost being fifty feet from your backdoor versus under your kitchen sink.

It's at times like these, though, that I like to remind people that your regular trash can already stinks. Compost is far more likely to offer you a solution to this problem than be its cause, and it's far more likely to smell good—like rich, damp earth—than bad, particularly if you provide it with a minimum of care. If you're balking at the perception of effort, still, all I can do is point out that your garbage already represents an exertion (how often are your schlepping bags to the basement for disposal by your building?), and that switching to compost might actually reduce your overall workload.

The first thing to do is assess your space. You and your future compost will mutually benefit from finding an out-of-the-way place for storage. Look to kitchen cabinets, closet shelves, balconies (!), and even beneath the bed. Anywhere you can find where you can stash a bag or a small plastic bucket. Then, assess yourself. How much food waste are you making? Do you live alone? Part of a couple? Do you have kids? The more food waste you make, the more space you'll want to make for your indoor compost. You might even take this opportunity to get rid of some stuff you forgot that you owned.

Now, settle on your set up.

You can buy a bokashi system, or a worm bucket. However, if you're like me, your preference will be the simple one-bag system that is outlined in *The Rodale Book of Composting*. The one-bag set up is squishier than a prebuilt system, and thus more easily stored (smush it under the sink or into a closet), and it can also be rigged from existing materials, and therefore costs basically nothing.

To build one, you'll need to start with a medium-sized plastic bag. If the bag is not self-sealing, you'll need a twist-tie. You will also need some kind of garden dirt, soil, or finished compost—about half as much as you have food scraps. Try to find this from a local garden or a friend's house versus buying a commercial product from a store. You could, in a pinch, even collect decaying, fallen leaves from some trees at the park. The goal here, after all, is to introduce a healthy set of active and happy microorganisms, so that we can kickstart decomposition. For the final touch, you'll need about a tablespoon of alfalfa meal or pellets. You can order this direct from a garden center, or you can find it at basically any pet store, where it's routinely labeled as "rabbit food." (Ha ha ha.)

To create your compost, chop your food scraps up into tiny, little pieces. Add them to the plastic bag. Add the garden soil or finished compost. If you collected leaves, add them—but make sure to crunch them up beforehand. Add your tablespoon of alfalfa. Add one ounce of tap water. Mix everything together. You can do this quite easily simply by closing the bag and giving it a good shake. Then, close your bag (but leave it plumped with a bit of air! your compost wants that oxygen), and stash it. From here, you'll want to gently squeeze and roll it once a day or so, in order to "mix" things. You'll also want to open the bag once or twice to week to "air it out" (a.k.a. introduce additional oxygen), which will allow for ongoing decomposition. Within four-to-six weeks, you'll have usable compost.

When I use this system, I usually get two bags going at once. That way, one bag is always "curing" (e.g. nothing new is being added, which allows the compost to reach a complete state of decomposition), and one bag is always active (e.g. able to have new material added to it). Similar to any other compost, you'll want to add things in proportion. For every cup of food scraps you add, toss in another tablespoon of alfalfa. If things in the bag are drying out, add a little bit of water. If they're too wet, add more alfalfa. You will not need to add more soil, as this ingredient was about introducing an initial microbe population and less about ongoing maintenance.

Most of all, trust yourself to figure it out.

Maintenance of a one-bag compost, for the most part, can be incorporated into your existing routine. Things will break down faster if they're added in smaller bits, so break stuff up as you add it. You can do this quite easily as part of usual meal preparation. Slice up your zucchini ends and your kale stems as you go. Add them to the bag when you're done. This will make it easier for your compost to digest them, and they'll break down more quickly.

VERMICOMPOST

Vermicompost is considered to be the richest, most nutrient-dense soil available for a farm or garden. Building your own vermicompost system is an easy and affordable way to make yourself a self-replenishing supply of this vital fertilizer.

First, a note on worms: not all worms are the same when it comes to compost. For vermicompost, red wigglers (the same kind you use when fishing) are the standard because they prefer to occupy the top 6 inches of soil. Other types of worms like to burrow deep, deep down and stay there, which makes them less likely to end up munching on your food scraps. You can buy a lot of red wigglers for not very much money at almost any garden or fishing store.

To build your own vermicompost, you will need:

— worms!
— two plastic storage tubs

- a drill
- cardboard, paper, old eggshell cartons (etc.)
- dirt or compost
- water
- food scraps

In general, when you build any vermicomposting system, you're really just making an ideal home for your worms. Worms love moisture and dislike sunlight. They need oxygen, and they prefer shadier and cooler areas. They need some type of "grit" in their surroundings that they can eat, which then helps them grind up and digest their food. Grit is a feature of most dirt, but if you want to be extra thorough, you can add oyster flour or rock dust. Only a little is needed—a tablespoon or so. These general principles are good to keep in mind as you build, and then nurture, their habitat.

To get started, you'll want to drill a series of holes in the bottom of one of your two plastic storage bins. A lot of 'em. These holes are there to provide good drainage, so the ooze that begins to leak from your decaying food scraps doesn't pool and drown your worms. You'll also be continually wetting your vermicompost in order to keep the environment moist, and the holes give the water someplace to go.

Next, you'll want to fill your newly-drilled bin with a mixture of bulky brown materials and dirt or compost. (We used compost because we had a lot of it on hand. Go figure.) For browns, we used old eggshell cartons and some paper grocery bags. Cardboard also works well, though. This material, when wet, retains moisture for the worms so that their environment stays damp, and it also provides aeration, so they have oxygen. That means you'll want your brown materials to be on the bulkier side, and to tear them into large-ish pieces.

Once you've filled the bottom 1/3 or so of the bin, you'll want to moisten everything. Use a hose and give it a good, long soak. The excess water will run out the bottom (remember! the holes...) and, if you have a dog, she'll also probably need a drink at this point. You want to wet the mixture until it's moist enough that you can squeeze a palm full and get drips of water coming out.

Next, you're going to add food scraps. Red wigglers will eat most things, including paper, poop, and coffee grounds. They will eat soft stuff first since they don't have teeth. You can help them out a little by chopping up your food scraps before you add them.

Add an equal amount of food scraps to your compost as dirt and cardboard. Mash it all up and wet it again if it needs it. Voila! You have created your worm bed, and now it's time to add your worms. Be gentle with them when you do. Nuzzle a hole into your worm bed, place them into it, and cover them up again. Then, find a good piece of cardboard and soak it in water. Place this over the top of your newly-built worm bed. It will help keep things dark and extra-moist.

Now, you will use your remaining storage bin as a catchment for your first bin's ooze. You can DIY this by simply placing some large-ish rocks or pieces of wood into the bottom of your second bin, and setting your first bin on top of them. This leaves some space between the two bins where liquid can pool, without drowning the worms.

Just remember to lift the first bin out and empty the liquid every once in a while. Cover your top bin, and find a cool and shady place to set everything.

From here, taking care of your worms is fairly simple. Keep in mind the principles sketched out at the beginning of this guide: worms need oxygen, moisture, and darkness. Make sure you're keeping your worm bed moist, and that you're adding new food scraps at the same rate your worms are consuming the old ones. If the brown material you've added starts to break down and the soil becomes compacted, wet and add some more (cardboard, eggshell cartons, whatever!), making sure to mix it in thoroughly. Like all things compost, your most important source of information is simply your attention.

When it comes time to use your vermicompost, you will recognize worm castings (e.g. worm poop, e.g. the vermicompost) because their texture is slightly different than the surrounding dirt or compost. You can reach in and grab a handful to use any time you want. If you grab a worm or two along with the castings, that's fine. They'll be very happy in your garden.

WHAT YOU SHOULDN'T COMPOST

California is home to nine species of oak: valley, blue oak, coast live, Engelmann, canyon live, interior live, black, island. and Oregon white. Together, these stooped giants drop a thick carpet of sturdy, carbon-rich leaf matter beneath their canopies, providing the soil with a slow decaying feast of critical nutrients.

Oak leaves can make for excellent compost. They're nutrient-dense, carbon-heavy powerhouses that many people will rake up and add to their backyard piles, something that feels akin to "cleaning up."

However, the orderly backyard is often created at the expense of ecological balance—and when you take oak leaves for your pile, you are definitively taking them from the oak tree. I often advise people to source inputs for their compost from their surroundings, but I also take pains to remind them that they're sharing those resources with their plant and animal neighbors.

The oak, specifically, really needs its leaves.

Oak trees count on their leaf litter for a number of reasons, like (one) nutrients, (two) enrichment of the soil surrounding their roots, and (three) the suppression of unfavorable plants ("weeds") that would disrupt their feeding and reproduction. Oaks are very sensitive to what plants they share space with. They thrive best alongside coastal sage scrub and chaparral, but these types of plant communities are vanishing and you're now more likely to find oaks surrounded by European grasses, especially in residential neighborhoods. As a result, oaks are dying across the state. Trees weakened by poor landscaping practices are less likely to flower and less likely to produce acorns. If acorns are produced, they're less likely to germinate and even less likely to successfully grow.

To understand the principle at play, it helps to understand a little more about how an oak "eats." Oaks are ectomycorrhizal, which means they utilize ectomycorrhizae (EcM) to help them find and intake nutrients. EcM forms a sheath around the root hairs of the oak, surrounding the cortical root cells, and then it goes searching for food. It reaches up into the oak's layer of leaf litter, where it is able to source small amounts of nutrients made available by the slowly decaying leaves and transfer them back to the oak. This is a clever and symbiotic survival strategy, but it also makes the oak highly vulnerable to soil disturbance around its roots. For example: from the removal of its fallen leaves, and the subsequent encroachment of invasively-behaving grasses that do not provide nutrients to the tree or (critically) its acorns.

If you have an oak in your yard, you may feel suddenly moved to rush out the store and purchase a commercially available mycorrhizal inoculant. I would caution you against this. Most inoculants are made of endomycorrhizae, which is a different type of differently-functioning mycorrhizae. You might also worry that you need to fertilize. Don't do this either. Introducing external, synthetic fertilizers will cause the oak to disconnect its (slowly-built) mycorrhizal relationships as it takes in a sudden excess of quickly available nutrition. You do not want to destroy that carefully built network. All you want to do is get out of its way, and let it do its thing.

So, as much as I love to compost everything in sight, I always recommend

                that you

    leave

your oak leaves

                      alone.

Open air compost (covered), 2021
Paper bags, loose grass, coffee grounds,
food scraps, flowers

COMPOST THIS BOOK

This book has been printed on recycled paper using soy ink (yes, even the parts in color!) and its pages will make for an excellent source of carbon in any compost pile. Its binding however, is made with non-biodegradable glue. Try as I might, I could not figure out a binding solution that was both truly biodegradable and cost-effective. Despite that, we will do our best.

To compost this book, I recommend first destroying it. Separate the pages from the binding. Discard the binding. Now shred the pages into pieces. You might go page-by-page. You might grab handfuls and rip. You might use scissors. You might even—and this is for the both courageous and safety-minded—burn the pieces and turn them into ash.

Next, you can begin your compost. Moisten the paper and mix it with food scraps. If you've burned your book into ash, pinch it with your fingers and sprinkle it throughout your pile. Or add it all at once, who cares?

The knowledge from this book lives in your head now. No, not knowledge. Let's call it permission. I hope that this book has been permission for you to try something and see what happens. Trust yourself to make mistakes and to learn from them.

Go on now, make compost.

CITATIONS
in *History* chapter

1. Plutarch. *Lives, Volume IX: Demetrius and Antony. Pyrrhus and Gaius Marius*. Translated by Bernadotte Perrin, Loeb Classical Library 101, Harvard University Press, 1920.

2. Lightfoot, John, and Robert Gandell. *Horae Hebraicae et Talmudicae: Hebrew and Talmudical Exercitations upon the Gospels, the Acts, Some Chapters of St. Paul's Epistle to the Romans, and the First Epistle to the Corinthians*. Oxford University Press, 1859.

3. Loewen, Jim. "The History of Composting in America." *History News Network*, George Washington University, 16 Dec. 2016, historynewsnetwork.org/blog/153202.

4. Adams, John. Diary 44, 27 March–21 July 1786 [electronic edition]. *Adams Family Papers: An Electronic Archive*, Massachusetts Historical Society, masshist.org/digitaladams.

FURTHER READING

Lal, Rattan. *The Love of Soil: Strategies to Regenerate Our Food Production Systems*. Chelsea Green Publishing, 2019.

Gershuny, Grace and Deborah L. Martin. *Rodale's Basic Organic Gardening: A Beginner's Guide to Starting a Healthy Garden*. Rodale Books, 2018.

Lowenfels, Jeff and Wayne Lewis. *Teaming with Microbes: The Organic Gardener's Guide to the Soil Food Web*. Timber Press, 2010.

Marsh, Andie. *Soil Is Sexy*. soilissexy.substack.com.

ABOUT THE AUTHOR

Photo by Amanda Hakan

Cassandra Marketos is a Los Angeles-based writer, compost practitioner, and community volunteer. She works in her neighborhood to divert food waste from landfills, maintain a community compost hub, and provide education on decay. Her work has appeared at Vielmetter Gallery, where she designed a compost pile from pieces of the gallery itself. You can read her reflections on compost and the philosophical implications of decomposition in her newsletter *The Rot*, at therot.substack.com.

Compost This Book
by Cassandra Marketos
is published by

Apogee Graphics
404 South Figueroa Street, Suite 518
Los Angeles, CA 90027
apogeegraphics.la

Publication © 2023 Apogee Graphics.

All rights reserved. No part of this book may be reproduced, stored in a retrieval system or transmitted in any form or by means electronic, mechanical, photocopying, recording, or otherwise, without the written permission of the publisher.

Designed by Apogee Graphics.

ISBN 979-8-9870855-3-0
LCCN 2023914396

Thanks to my grandmother, who was the first to make me love books. And thanks to CJN and WITI for being the first to coach my love of compost into public view.